Peter Coker RA

NEW WORK 2002

with an Introduction by

FRANCES SPALDING

Paul Holberton publishing

LONDON

Peter Coker RA

NEW WORK 2002

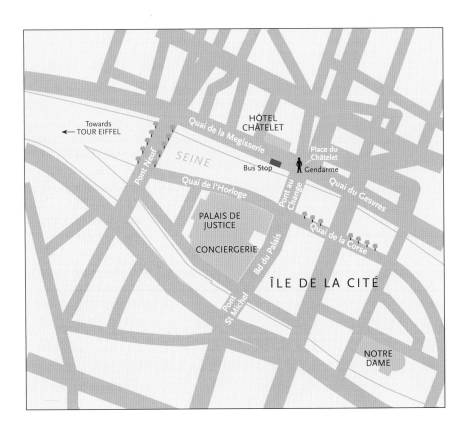

First published 2003
Produced by Paul Holberton publishing
37 Snowsfields, London SE1 3SU
www.paul-holberton.net

British Library Cataloguing in Publication Data
A catalogue record for this book is available from the British Library

ISBN 1 903470 15 3

Front cover: Detail, *Paris at Night from the Hôtel Châtelet III* (oil over lithograph)
Back cover: *Chaos* (from *The Parisian Suite*)
Frontispiece: Detail, *Pont au Change, Paris*

Designed by Philip Lewis
Map by ML Design

Printed in Italy

Preface

PETER COKER

ON A VISIT TO PARIS with my son in the 1970s I made a number of drawings from a second-floor window of the Hôtel Châtelet, looking right, left and dead ahead over the Pont au Change, a noisy and vibrant junction with the Quai de la Megisserie, involving traffic, bus queues, pedestrians and the general chaos of busy Parisian life during both day and night. This impression of vigour and activity has remained with me since that time and it is this element that I have tried to retain.

These 1970s drawings (see pages 6, 7 and 12) have been stored away for nearly three decades, until comparatively recently. The sight of them released an explosion of pent-up creativity that since my stroke in 1990 I had thought would not be possible.

The result has been a number of large oils, crayon and oil-pastel drawings, etchings and lithographs, plus two architectural drawings in charcoal and black and white chalk of the Pont au Change from the Quai de l'Horloge. The last two drawings were made from a sanguine study of an earlier date (page 11).

These works of Paris were all made in a short space of time, April to December 2002. Exploring the interrelationships of various media led to works in oil, watercolour and oil pastel, and to etchings and, for the first time, lithography. Every medium creates its own response, problem and solution. Curwen's lithographic colour proofs stimulated my use of fractured translucent glazes and solid oil paint over four selected proofs, developing a more intense sense of night and of general chaos (see pages 29–32). The entire movement back and forth from one medium to another created, through experimentation, vitality and directness of statement.

The progress was as follows: by the end of April I had made tentative efforts to start painting and had produced two small oils and three or four mixed media works (see pages 14–18). These were a prelude to the first major oil painting, *Pont au Change, Paris* (28″ × 48″; page 22), made directly from the 1970s drawing of the same subject (overleaf, upper left). *Paris at Night from the Hôtel Châtelet* (page 23) followed from the 1970s black Chinese ink-and-wash drawing (page 7, lower right), which stimulated, to my surprise, a highly coloured, vibrant interpretation. This led to further experimentation.

I had long wanted to publish a suite of etchings and the linear content of the 1970s drawings suggested etching as a means of expression.

Pont au Change, Paris
Pen, ink, watercolour and gouache
14″ × 23½″

Double Arch towards the Boulevard du Palais
Pen, ink and wash
14″ × 12″

Configuration
Ink and wash, 14½″ × 10½″

**Pedestrians crossing the Quai
de la Megisserie**
Chinese ink
14¹/₄″ × 10¹/₂″

Gendarme facing the Quai de Gesvres
Chinese ink
15″ × 10¹/₂″

Cars crossing the Pont au Change
Pencil
14¹/₄″ × 9¹/₂″

Chaos
Chinese ink and watercolour
14¹/₂″ × 11³/₄″

Paris, Night
Pen, Chinese ink and wash
14″ × 11³/₄″

Working from a wheelchair made the physical process impossible without the assistance of a technician. Linda Richardson, an artist printmaker, was willing to undertake this task and, working together from August to December 2002, we produced *The Parisian Suite* (see pages 36–47).

The black drawing *Paris, Night* seemed to lend itself to lithography rather than to etching (see page 7, lower right, and page 47). The oil painting *Paris at Night from the Hôtel Châtelet* (page 23) stimulated a lithograph, as did the drawing *Pont au Change, Paris* (page 6).

The three lithographs were printed by the Curwen Studio from September to November 2002 and are limited to editions of 25 prints.

1   *Paris, Night*, image size 14″ × 11³/₄″
    Printed in three colours on Velin Arches Blanc 250 gsm,
    hand torn to 26″ × 22″ (included in *The Parisian Suite*)

2   *Pont au Change, Paris*, image size 14″ × 23¹/₂″
    Printed in eight colours on Somerset Velvet 300 gsm,
    hand torn to 21¹/₂″ × 29″

3   *Paris at Night from the Hôtel Châtelet*
    Printed in twelve colours on Somerset Velvet 300 gsm,
    hand torn to 32″ × 27″

The colour proofs of *Paris at Night from the Hôtel Châtelet* suggested further experimentation in December 2002.

I was amused to find in Tate Britain's superb catalogue for the 'Constable to Delacroix' exhibition in 2003 Thomas Carlyle's observation: "To live in Paris for a fortnight is a treat; to live in it continually would be a martyrdom".

Have things changed, I wonder?

2002	WATERCOLOURS, DRAWINGS, MIXED MEDIA	OILS	LITHOGRAPHS	ETCHINGS
April	*Gendarme at the Châtelet* 19″ × 24″ *Double Arch, Pont au Change* 22″ × 23¹/₂″ *Towards Notre Dame from the Pont au Change* 14¹/₂″ × 9¹/₂″	*Chaos, Châtelet* on board 14″ × 9¹/₂″ *Bus Stop, Châtelet* 20″ × 16″		
May	*From the Window, Hôtel Châtelet* 11″ × 8″ *Night, Pont au Change* 11″ × 8″ *From the Window of the Hôtel Châtelet* 21¹/₂″ × 24¹/₂″ *The Pont au Change towards the Place du Châtelet* 30″ × 20″ (from a pencil-and-sanguine study of unknown date, 14″ × 14″)	*The Pont au Change, Paris* 28″ × 48″ (from 1970s drawing)		
July–August		*Paris at Night from the Hôtel Châtelet* 48″ × 42″ (from black 1970s Chinese ink drawing) *The Pont au Change at Night* 48″ × 36″ (from drawing made in May)		
August–December				*The Parisian Suite:* 1. *Cars crossing the Pont au Change* 2. *Chaos* 3. *Gendarme facing the Quai de Gesvres* 4. *Bus Stop, Châtelet* 5. *Bus Stop, Châtelet* 6. *Pedestrians crossing the Quai de la Megisserie* 7. *Double Arch, towards the Bd du Palais* 8. *Double Arch, towards the Bd du Palais* 9. *Configuration* 10. *Paris, Night*
September–October		*Double Arch, Pont au Change* 40″ × 32″ (from 1970s ink-and-wash *Double Arch*) *Towards the Pont Neuf from the Hôtel Châtelet* 40″ × 34″		
September–November			*Paris, Night* Printed in 3 colours 14″ × 11³/4″ *The Pont au Change, Paris* Printed in 8 colours 14″ × 23¹/₂″ *Paris at Night from the Hôtel Châtelet* Printed in 12 colours 32″ × 27″	
November–December	*The Pont au Change from the Quai de l'Horloge* Pastel and charcoal over grey lithographic paper, 32″ × 27″	*Paris at Night from the Hôtel Châtelet I–III* Oil over lithograph 32″ × 27″ *Night towards the Tour Eiffel* Oil over lithograph 34″ × 27″ *The Pont Neuf from the Hôtel Châtelet* 48″ × 34″ *Configuration* 30″ × 25″		

Peter Coker's return to Paris

FRANCES SPALDING

OF ALL THE EPISODES within Peter Coker's long career, none is
more surprising than the recent explosion of creativity, following
a difficult time of illness. As Coker himself describes in the preface,
a major stimulus was the build up of frustration during a period of
inactivity as a painter. Artists, of course, are to some extent always
working – processing experience, thinking, looking, feeling, reading.
That we all need to pause is a piece of common sense. But a curious
paradox can attend the business of waiting in those instances
when, to paraphrase T.S. Eliot, we go by way of dispossession –
what we are not – and in the course of that unmaking or unravelling
something new or different emerges. The form that it took in this
particular case was an imaginative return to a corner of Paris.

'Corner' is perhaps an inappropriate word to use of the busy
intersection outside the Hôtel Châtelet. Here Coker stayed with his
son in the mid 1970s, making a cluster of drawings of what he
could see in three different directions. Within his range were two
bridges marching across the Seine, also the sweep of the Quai de la
Megisserie which passed below and away into the distance. Within
the larger configurations smaller incidents occurred: a small crowd
gathered at a bus stop; people tramped the pavements and across
the Pont au Change; and a *gendarme* stood at the interchange
endeavouring to conduct the traffic.

Ever since Baudelaire, in a famous essay which he published in
1863, praised the spectacle offered by Paris and called for a 'painter
of modern life', artists have repeatedly found inspiration in the
fabric and texture of this great city. Even Mondrian, after he had
rigorously excluded representation from his art, was sufficiently
entranced by Paris to compose in words two vignettes of urban life.
He was working on the first, 'Les Grands Boulevards', while his
friend Van Doesburg was staying, as the latter recorded in a letter
to J.J.P. Oud: "This noon, happily, we were on the Boulevard
des Capucines, where we observed the working of the incredible
machine that is Paris. It was a beautiful spring day, and we sat
outdoors. One could cross the Place de l'Opera only with the
greatest caution, but Mondrian did it as calmly as if he were in his
atelier. The beauty [of Paris] is that it is so spontaneous, unplanned,
whereas what is intentional is for the most part baroque, overladen."[1]

1 Quoted in *The New Art – The New Life: The Collected Writings of Piet Mondrian*,
  edited and translated by Harry Holtzman and Martin S.James (Thames &
  Hudson, 1987), p.124

Pencil and Sanguine Study
Pencil and sanguine, 14″ × 14″

Coker's 1970s drawings convey a similar fascination with order and chaos, movement and stillness, anonymity and grandeur. The eye glides over bridges, along pavements or up the diminishing vista of a street punctuated with figures and the counter-movement of a pedestrian crossing. This experience of the city in terms of space, speed and interruption is, in Coker's drawings, translated into pictorial equivalents which encourage the eye to jump, slide and travel around the page. The handling is decisive, cursory and abrupt. It provides enough information for the viewer to recognise and imaginatively inhabit the scene portrayed, but at the same time the pictorial illusion is always held in tension with an awareness of the drawing's material attributes, its existence as a series of marks or washes on the paper surface. It is this double life that gives these drawings their vitality and urgency.

They did not, at the time, generate paintings. But on rediscovering them, almost three decades later, Coker immediately began trying to recreate, both in small oils and in crayon and oil-pastel drawings, the vigour and energy of these scenes. Though he refers to some of the early works in this series as 'tentative', they all contain a fierce passion and a directness which gives his work its stylistic

Figures crossing the Bridge (Pont au Change)
Chinese ink and watercolour
$10^1/_2'' \times 14^3/_4''$

signature. The ingredients in *Bus Stop, Châtelet* emerge shaken
and tumbling. When he focuses on a smaller knot of interest,
as in *Chaos*, the arrangement becomes more tightly clenched,
conveying something of the excitement which can also be found
in the 1970s drawing, *Figures crossing the Bridge (Pont au Change)*.

Three or four months after these early paintings began, Coker
produced his first major oil in this new series, *Pont au Change,
Paris*. Like the 1970s drawing on which it is based, it plays on the
three-way junction set up by the meeting of the bridge with the
quai: this both draws us in to the picture and then sets up a
tension between the two vanishing points which travel outwards
and swing the eye from one side of the picture to the other. Here,
and in all these Parisian scenes, the reminting of experience offers
the viewer a wonderfully invigorating set of sensations. What is
astonishing is that though these paintings have been produced
from a wheelchair, with all the awkwardnesses and irritations this
must involve, they convey a marvellous sense of physical vitality.

Coker's work has always contained an astringent freshness of
perception: it disrupts visual complacency, and continues to do so
in this new series of paintings and prints. But even the artist himself
was surprised by the painting he produced after looking at an earlier
wash drawing of the river view at night. *Paris at Night from the
Hôtel Châtelet* is built up out of a ragged cluster of strongly coloured
brushmarks, which have eddied together like driftwood left behind

by the tide. The rich colours are made still more vibrant by the white ground which breaks through with crystalline effect and by the deep blue-black in the sky. The final image is deeply evocative, but more of a mnemonic than a representation, topography having dissolved into a distant but highly charged reminiscence.

Coker's preface describes how this and another painting, *Pont au Change, Paris*, gave rise to lithographs. Before this development occurred, his desire to see his 1970s drawings translated into a series of etchings had already reawakened his interest in the medium of print. Working with an artist-printmaker proved to be a major stimulation behind this new work; and the business of seeing ideas cross from one medium into another allowed new ideas and interrelationships to be uncovered in the process. However, Coker's most productive period of experimentation seems to have occurred towards the end of 2002, in a burst of activity that brought this new work to a climax.

Part of the success of *Paris at Night from the Hotel Châtelet* is that, while suggesting darkness and depth, it simultaneously lies so well on the surface of the canvas. This in itself may have invited its translation into lithography by Curwen Studios. On being shown the final lithographic colour proofs of this image, Coker asked if he could retain some of the trial printings, and on these he began adding both thin glazes and solid touches of paint. As he mentions in the preface, he wanted to see if he could heighten still further the sense of night and urban chaos. The initial two proofs that he worked on developed a dark, sombre quality, the reds turning a rich magenta and deep, dusky brown-greys appearing in the sky. Then, in the next and final pair, the mood changed again, as the sky lightened, owing to the introduction of a deep blue and a purple, which now became the predominant hues. These seem to have encouraged a more exuberant palette to float over the armature supplied by the underlying lithographic print. The resulting image carries a rich weight of colour with a paradoxical lightness. Coker recollects having the sudden awareness that, whereas before he had always been sharply conscious of what could or could not be done in a picture, he was now working without regard for anything other than the sheer pleasure in the activity of painting. As a result these two last versions convey an extraordinary sense of freedom and release, a glorious delight in the affirmative and life-enhancing power of paint, mark and colour.

New Work 2002

Gendarme at the Châtelet
Mixed media on paper, 19″ × 24″

Double Arch, Pont au Change
Mixed media on paper, 22″ × 23½″

Towards Notre Dame from the Pont au Change
Pencil, ink and watercolour on paper, 14¹/₂″ × 9¹/₂″

Chaos, Châtelet
Oil on board, 14″ × 9¹/₂″

Bus Stop, Châtelet
Oil on canvas, 20″ × 16″

From the Window, Hôtel Châtelet
Wax crayon and oil pastel with turps wash on paper, 11 × 8″

Night, Pont au Change
Wax crayon and oil pastel with turps wash on paper, 11″ × 8″

From the Window of the Hôtel Châtelet
Mixed media on paper, 21^1/$_2$″ × 24^1/$_2$″

Pont au Change, Paris
Oil on canvas, 28″ × 48″

Paris at Night from the Hôtel Châtelet
Oil on canvas, 48″ × 42″

The Pont au Change towards the Place du Châtelet
Charcoal, chalk and pastel on paper, 30″ × 20″

The Pont au Change at Night
Oil on canvas, 48″ × 36″

Double Arch, Pont au Change
Oil on canvas, 40" × 32"

Towards the Pont Neuf from the Hôtel Châtelet
Oil on canvas, 40″ × 34″

Paris at Night from the Hôtel Châtelet
Lithograph printed in 12 colours, 32″ × 27″

Paris at Night from the Hôtel Châtelet I
Oil over lithograph, 32″ × 27″

Paris at Night from the Hôtel Châtelet II
Oil over lithograph, 32″ × 27″

Paris at Night from the Hôtel Châtelet III
Oil over lithograph, 32″ × 27″

Night towards the Tour Eiffel
Oil over lithograph, 34″ × 27″

The Pont au Change from the Quai de l'Horloge
Pastel and charcoal over grey lithographic paper, 32" × 27"

The Pont Neuf from the Hôtel Châtelet
Oil on canvas, 48″ × 34″

Configuration
Oil on canvas, 30″ × 25″

The Parisian Suite

A series of soft ground etchings and aquatints, frontispiece and description, each edition limited to 25 prints numbered and signed, plus 5 artist's proofs, 1 printer's proof, 2 etchings hand coloured by the artist and 2 tinted by Linda Richardson who proofed and printed the editions.

This series is accompanied by a lithograph printed by The Curwen Studio.

Printed on Fabriano Tiepolo 290 gsm 100% cotton mould-made paper, size 26"x22", each sheet bears the printer's chop mark bottom right corner and watermark Fabriano Tiepolo to the left. Etched on copper plates— soft ground etching/aquatint. Plate size given in inches.

Frontispiece, 15¾"x0¾". Aquatint.

1. Cars crossing the Pont au Change, 15¾"x11¾". Line etching.
2. Chaos, 16"x12". Line + aquatint, hand coloured by the artist.
3. Gendarme facing the Quai de Gesvres, 15¾"x0¾". Line + aquatint.
4. Bus stop, Châtelet, 14"x13¾". Line + aquatint, hand tinted.
5. Bus stop, Châtelet, 16"x13¾". Line + aquatint.
6. Pedestrians crossing the Quai de la Mégisserie, 15¾"x11¾". Line + aquatint, hand coloured by the artist.
7. Double arch, towards the Bd du Palais, 14"x12½". — Line + aquatint, hand tinted.
8. Double arch, towards the Bd du Palais, 14"x12½". Line + aquatint.
9. Configuration, 15¾"x0¾". Aquatint.
10. Paris, night, 4"x11⅞". Lithograph, printed on Velin Arches Blanc 270 gsm.

Ap ⅕

Peter Coker.

Handwritten Description
(lithographically produced)

Frontispiece
15³/₄" × 11³/₄". Aquatint

Cars crossing the Pont au Change
15³/₄″ × 11³/₄″. Line etching

Chaos
14″ × 12″. Line and aquatint,
hand coloured by the artist

Gendarme facing the Quai de Gesvres
15³/₄″ × 11³/₄″. Line and aquatint

Bus Stop, Châtelet
14″ × 13¾″. Line and aquatint, hand tinted

Bus stop, Châtelet
14″ × 13³/4″. Line and aquatint

Pedestrians crossing the Quai de la Megisserie
15³/₄″ × 11³/₄″. Line and aquatint, hand coloured by the artist

Double Arch, towards the Bd du Palais
14″ × 12¹/₂″. Line and aquatint, hand tinted

Double Arch, towards the Bd du Palais
14″ × 12½″. Line and aquatint

Configuration
15³/₄″ × 11³/₄″. Aquatint

Paris, Night
14″ × 11³/₄″. Lithograph

Acknowledgements

I would like to thank Linda Richardson, artist printmaker; Stanley Jones and Jenny Roland of the Curwen Studio; Frances Spalding, art historian, critic and biographer; Douglas Atfield, photographer; Nelson Blowers, framer; and finally Andrew Hunter, curator of the exhibition, and the Trustees of Gainsborough's House

Peter Coker 2003

This publication has been printed privately for Peter Coker to accompany the exhibition *Peter Coker RA: New Work* at Gainsborough's House, Sudbury, 12 July–7 September 2003.

Produced by Paul Holberton publishing in an edition of one thousand copies, of which two hundred and fifty have been numbered and signed by the artist to be sold in aid of Gainsborough's House.

Peter Coker RA

Born London 1926; Odhams Press and St Martin's School of Art, part-time 1941–43; Fleet Air Arm 1943–46; St Martin's School of Art 1947–50; Royal College of Art 1950–54; Royal Scholarship 1951; married Vera Crook 1951; son Nicholas born 1952; British Institution Scholarship 1953; moved from London to Mistley, Essex 1962; elected Associate of the Royal Academy 1965; elected Royal Academician 1972; taught painting, part-time, at St Martin's School of Art 1954–73 and at City and Guilds London Art School 1973–85; son Nicholas died 1985

ONE-MAN EXHIBITIONS

Zwemmer Gallery, London 1956/57/59/64/67; Magdalene Street Gallery, Cambridge 1968; Stone Gallery, Newcastle 1969; Thackeray Gallery, London 1970/72/74/75/76/78; Retrospective tour : Colchester, Bath, London, Sheffield 1972–73; Retrospective, Chelmsford and Essex Museum 1978; Paintings and Drawings of the Butcher's Shop, Royal Academy, London and touring 1979; Gallery 10, Grosvenor Street, London 1980/82/84/86/88; Working Drawings and Sketchbooks (1955 to 1988), Fitzwilliam Museum, Cambridge 1989; Flying Colours Gallery, Edinburgh 1990/91; Textile Designs (1954 to 1956), Mayor Gallery, London 1991; Landscapes (1955 to 1991), touring: Kendal, London, Carlisle and Ipswich 1992/93; 75th Birthday Display, Tate Britain, 2001; Major Retrospective (1949 to 1992), Chris Beetles Gallery, London 2002

SELECTED GROUP EXHIBITIONS

Young Contemporaries 1949/51; Royal Academy Summer Exhibition 1950 to present day; 'The Artist's View of an Industry', Shell Petroleum Company Ltd 1954; 'Looking Forward', South London Art Gallery 1956; Contemporary Art Society, 'Religious Theme', Tate Gallery 1958; 'British Artists', Jordan Galleries, Toronto 1958; 'Recent Acquisitions', Contemporary Art Society 1959; John Moores, Liverpool 1959/61; 'Das junge England, Europäisches Forum', Alpbach 1960; Neue Galerie der Stadt, Linz, Austria 1960; 'British Painting 1950–57', Arts Council of Great Britain 1962; 'Towards Art ?', 1952–62, Royal College of Art 1962; 'Bicentenary Exhibition 1768–1968', Royal Academy of Arts, London 1968; 'Painting 1950–57', Scottish Arts Council, Glasgow 1969; 'British Painting 1900–1960', Sheffield and Aberdeen Art Galleries 1975–76; 'British Painting 1952–1977', Royal Academy of Arts, London 1977; Recent Chantrey Purchases, Tate Gallery 1981; Acquisitions since 1980, Tate Gallery 1982; 'The Forgotten Fifties', touring exhibition 1984; 'New Twentieth Century Acquisitions', National Portrait Gallery 1986; 'Exhibition Road: Painters at the Royal College of Art', London 1988; 'The Kitchen Sink Painters', Mayor Gallery, London 1991; New Displays, Tate Gallery 1992

PUBLIC COLLECTIONS

Arts Council of Great Britain; Victoria Art Gallery, Bath; Bagshaw Art Gallery, Batley; Birmingham City Museums and Art Gallery; Eastern Arts Association, Cambridge; Fitzwilliam Museum, Cambridge; Carlisle Museum and Art Gallery; Chelmsford and Essex Museum; The Minories, Colchester; Contemporary Art Society of Wales; Herbert Art Gallery, Coventry; Doncaster Museum and Art Gallery; Scottish National Gallery of Modern Art, Edinburgh; Ipswich Museums and Galleries; Abbot Hall Art Gallery, Kendal; Kettering Art Gallery; City Art Gallery, Leeds; Leicester Museums and Art Gallery; Walker Art Gallery, Liverpool; British Museum, London; Contemporary Art Society, London; Chantrey Bequest; National Maritime Museum, London; National Portrait Gallery, London; Royal Academy of Arts, London; Royal College of Art, London; Tate, London; Victoria and Albert Museum, London; City Art Gallery, Manchester; Norwich Castle Museum; Rugby Art Gallery and Museum; Rochdale Art Gallery and Museum; Salford Museum and Art Gallery; Sheffield City Art Galleries; Beecroft Art Gallery, Southend-on- Sea; Atkinson Art Gallery, Southport; Stedelijk Museum, Ostend; The Berardo Collection, Lisbon, Portugal

PUBLICATION

Etching Techniques, B.T. Batsford Ltd., London 1976

BIOGRAPHY

Peter Coker R.A., fully illustrated biography and catalogue raisonné, published by Chris Beetles Ltd, Ryder Street, St James's, London, 2002